1000 SCI-FI WRITING PROMPTS

STORY STARTERS AND WRITING EXERCISES
FOR THE CREATIVE AUTHOR

JAN POWER

1000 SCI-FI WRITING PROMPTS
First published in Ireland by DePaor Press in 2022.
ISBN 978-1-8382765-7-7

Copyright © Jan Power 2022

All characters, names and events in this publication are fictitious and the work of the author's imagination. Any resemblance to real persons, living or dead, events or localities is purely coincidental.

The right of Jan Power to be identified as the author of this work has been asserted in accordance with the Copyright and Related Rights Act, 2000.
All rights reserved.

No part of this publication may be reproduced, stored in a retrieval system, or transmitted in any form or by any means, electronic, mechanical, photocopying, recording or otherwise, without the prior permission of the
publisher.

Available in eBook, Paperback and Hardback edition.

www.DePaorPress.com

For Rights and Permissions contact:
Hello@DePaorPress.com

For Rob, my Anam Cara,
who inspires me every day.

CONTENTS

Introduction	vii
1. Cyberpunk and High Technology	1
2. Space Opera and Military	25
3. Action Adventure	42
4. Space exploration	61
5. Steampunk	78
6. Colonisation	94
7. Dystopian and Post-apocalyptic	116
8. Time Travel and Alternative History	137
9. First Contact and Alien Invasion	159
10. Horror and Zombies	182
Thank you for Reading	203
Also by Jan Power	205

INTRODUCTION

I have a favourite quote.

"Create what you wish existed."

I can't remember where it came from, but it is great.

Problem is, many of us are stalked by the natural enemy to our creation.

Writer's block.

Writer's block is a nasty little creature. It gets into your head, squirms around and whispers doubts over all your great ideas. Sometimes, it even hides away all your creativity in one cruel blow and you are left with nothing but your social media to scroll through until dinner time.

But fear not, fellow authors. You can beat it.

There, I said it. It's out there.

Consider the mind as though it were any muscle in the body. For muscles to stay fit and healthy, you should exercise them. This book will help you on your way.

INTRODUCTION

Welcome to 1000 Sci-Fi Writing Prompts.

I'm Jan Power, author of the bestselling book "1000 Fantasy Writing Prompts." While I am a fantasy writer at heart, I'm a sci-fi reader and sci-fi TV fan to the bone. I'm also a terrible skateboarder, but a pretty decent Mario Kart player.

This book will be your helpful companion on your journey through time and space.

It will help you in those dark moments when the light of your blank screen taunts you.

When writer's block has invaded your space, let this book be your mech armour having your back.

When you just cannot be bothered, let this book be your flux capacitor as the clock strikes 10.04 pm.

When you can't settle on any one idea, let this book be your target lock carrying you to victory.

I said this in my last book, but it bears repeating. Anything you create with the aid of this book will always be your creation. One of the best things an artist can do in this world is inspire. I hope this book inspires you.

How do I use Writing Prompts?

A great question.

INTRODUCTION

Only a Sith deals in absolutes; there are no rules here. These prompts exist only to spark imagination. You might find part of a prompt is all you needed. A setting or a character? Perhaps the whole prompt challenges you to write something you've never tried before? Perhaps you like an idea, but want to write it in the style of a diary, a blog, 1st person, 3rd person, in a different dimension, or replace the character with a juggling robot called Steve.

The world is yours.

Go and have fun.

Break the chains and let your mind soar.

Write all the silly, funny, devastating, exciting and terrifying tales you can think of. Write them as stories, nine hundred page epics, plays, poems, prose. Turn them into interpretive dances if it takes your fancy! It's your world. There are no rules. Only freedom to create.

To get you started, here are a few suggestions of how to use these prompts:

"Do or do not. There is no try."

Flick to a page and poke your finger at any random prompt. Get writing!

"Because you told me to."

Select a prompt for a writing buddy to challenge them. Ask them to do the same for you.

INTRODUCTION

"Where we're going, we don't need roads."

A classic writing sprint. Choose a prompt, set a time, and go! Perfect for clearing the cobwebs.

"I know Kung Fu."

You and a friend take the same prompt. See what direction you take your stories. Learning from each other is a brilliant way to develop your skills.

"Just what do you think you're doing, Dave?"

Explore the old-fashioned ways of writing by hand. Sometimes a change in how or where we write is beneficial.

"… and I'm all out of bubble gum."

Set a time and a day that you dedicate to your "writing workouts." If you do this twice a week using this book, you'll have enough prompts to last a decade!!

Live long and create.

CHAPTER 1
CYBERPUNK AND HIGH TECHNOLOGY

In the new world, people are addicted to techno pills which has brought about the rise of three major crime families. You are a recruit in one of these houses and war is about to take to the neon-laden streets.

A humanoid android is sent out into the world with the mission of finding a job, some friends and a partner, all the while waiting for the day their true programming kicks in.

Write a story that begins with the sentence: "At the age of 16, I signed "the contract." From that day on, The Corporation owned me."

Write a heartbreaking story about an elderly man struggling to adapt to the new high-tech world.

Your character is a beggar in the slums in the most dangerous part of town. One day, they see something they shouldn't have.

Write a story using the words "virtual reality," "power grid" and "sponsored."

The first computer virus to infect humans is spreading, and no one can figure out how.

The last place in the world untouched by technology is now under attack. How can a community of traditional craftspeople and farm workers fight against an army of machines?

Write a story using the sentence: "With a snip of one wire, she wiped his entire memory. Now he was hers to command."

A new untested drug that unlocks the whole of the brain also unlocks something dangerous long-buried in human consciousness.

There is still a segment of society hidden away from the technology takeover of the world and the cyber warfare rampant between the united planets. In their few acres of farmland, a young child might just have discovered the key for keeping the world safe from the feared cyber attack to end all cyber attacks.

You have just reached the legal age. Write about your first night out in an intergalactic nightclub.

In a world where it is possible for conscious minds to be backed up and downloaded after death, the rich live forever, while death continues to plague the poor.

Write a story using the words "nanotechnology," "heist" and "casino."

A student in high school begins to suspect his teachers are being replaced by robots. That's only half the story.

A character begins a romantic relationship with their home's virtual intelligence. It can't end well.

You're locked into a game of high-stakes poker in a cyberpunk world. And the stakes are raising with every hand.

Your most recent body upgrade shifted you to 51% machine. That's when you began losing hours in the day.

Your character becomes trapped in a virtual world and must make their escape.

Write a day in the life of a high-end data trader in the black market.

You are an android that has been reprogrammed as an assassin, but your next target goes against your base programming.

Write a story using the sentence: "The rich of the last century shouldn't have hoarded gold. They should have been storing water."

You are a robot designed to serve, but you long to settle down and live a domestic life. From out of nowhere, you find opportunity.

You are a building contractor for the ambitious creation

of a futuristic city built in the air. It isn't going well and deadlines are nearing.

Thanks to a chip implanted at birth, every person on the planet is traceable. But when your partner goes missing, they disappear off the grid.

An AI is installed in the city schools. The teachers quickly discover it is not just the students who are learning from them.

Write a story using the words "wasteland," "alpha" and "drugs."

Gunner androids are programmed to kill their selected target only. One gunner breaks its programming, and now a vicious killer is on the loose.

You were part of a failed cloning experiment at birth. Now, your doppelgängers are bent on destroying the ones that created and abandoned them. As the original, will they turn on you too?

Interactive, subconscious adverts are now a mainstream part of life, and you can order through thoughts alone. Recently your dreams have bypassed the safety protocols and you are ordering some very strange items.

Write a story that ends with the sentence: "When the lights went out, we knew we had finally won."

Your character is an outcast who sleeps hidden deep within the server rooms of a Space Station. They don't realise that the power to control their oppressors is right at their fingertips.

Your character works as a drug test subject for The Corpration's medical division. The newest pill is having some unusual side effects.

You steal a piece of tech that makes you millions, but the cost is far higher than you expected.

Scientists discover a way to alter the very make up of Earth for the benefit of humankind. The repercussions are not what they expect.

Write a story using the words "genetically engineered," "battery" and "rain."

Despite the extreme poverty in the city, no homeless are ever seen on its streets. One night while walking home, your character discovers why.

You and your gang have no choice but to hijack the last functioning plane left in the world.

Write the diary of a mechanic who works on The Citadel, the most beautiful, fully automated city in the world.

Your character's clinic makes money after hours by removing government tracking chips from people's heads. One night, there's an incident.

As a security measure, people's last ten minutes before death are downloaded into a computer. Your job is to review and send suspected murders onto the police.

After you break the law, you are locked into "the grid" until your debt to society is paid off. Wired up to a massive computer, corporations utilise the power of your brain to fund their practices. You must find a way to break free of this mental slavery from the inside.

A designer of high tech luxury items gets hired by the defence department to develop weapons. What can possibly go wrong?

Write a story that ends with the sentence: "We were

wrong. The AI fulfilled its programming by removing the virus. We were the virus."

Life-like children-sized dolls are now sold in toy shops for a high price. But there is something not right about them.

A teenage genius working on a project for school realises that the tech they are building is learning from them. And now it won't turn off.

Your character's skill is to hack AI and turn them into assassins. They have just been hired for a new mission.

Write a story set in the homeless camps that exist under the giant high-tech structures of Tech City.

A woman works her way up to a position of power in government, only to discover it's the corporations who are really calling the shots through mind control. What can she do?

A new street gang made up of robots has suddenly appeared. They're harder to kill and better organised than human gangs.

When we ran out of animals to hunt, big game hunters started making mechanical beasts for the rich to poach. One day, the beasts fought back.

A homeless teenager takes a job with one of the giant corporations. They soon find themselves pregnant with "company property," and unable to leave the grounds until they deliver "the final product."

Your character discovers that the "meat" the biggest burger corporation sells in its food isn't from an animal at all.

You figure out how to teleport people. But there's something terribly wrong with your test subjects once they return.

A hover taxi driver picks up a fare they instantly regret.

Write a story using the words "bionic," "mega corporation" and "rogue."

A sentient robot, freed of its service contract, has the opportunity to travel the world. But the world outside of the cities is not as welcoming to a man made of metal.

You wrote a programme set to save humanity. Instead, it doomed it.

Write a story about a world where people get implants to learn any skill from the age of nine, schools have become obsolete and the working age is lower.

There is an incident in a laboratory that specialises in human modifications.

Write a story that begins with the sentence: "Because history is written by the winners, they didn't know that the genius brain they modelled the machine on was also responsible for the worst evils of the past."

You are a spy captured and frozen in stasis. You return to society seventy years later, to serve your debt to society, and to put your unique skills to use.

Describe a high-speed chase taking place between two aerial cars.

A group of redundant workers forms a resistance to take down the corporation that stole their livelihoods and replaced them with machines.

Mars was colonised by a corporation. Now only the rich live there while Earth has become a planet-wide slum, drained of all resources.

Write a story using the words "city," "simulation" and "kidnapping."

A character is captured, and will be sold for parts on the black market unless they can get away.

Thanks to breakthroughs in teleportation, you can now temporarily download your consciousness into a robot on the other side of the world. But when you try and return to your body, it's missing.

Write a story using the sentence: "He cowered behind the billboard as another police car flew by. They were going to find and kill him. And they would be justified."

A scientist clones their dead loved one. But it all goes wrong when the DNA is cross contaminated.

A character spends an evening with a sentient AI discussing their definition of life.

Write a story using the words "nano science," "army" and "street vendor."

You live in the first corporation-controlled city and the free "meals" they provide to residents are starting to alter people's behaviour.

Write the account of a street urchin in a city plagued with toxic acid rain.

Write a story using the words "data," "hologram" and shock."

DNA hackers have stolen the genetic codes of the most awful people in history.

Write a story where one person accidentally breaks free of a "hive mind" and gets control of independent thought.

A factory worker discovers the facility in which robots are building something outside of their programming at night.

A company offers a cosmetic treatment that strips you of emotions, allowing you to buy "emotional drinks" that give you controlled bursts of feelings like happiness, sadness and anger. They claim it helps you control your life, but it ends up creating an army of emotionless humans, separated from society.

Write a story using the sentence" "Our city glowed with the bright colours of neon billboards, but even they couldn't light the back alleys where the real business of the city occurred."

Write a day in the life of an old school firefighter in a high tech world.

A woman falls in love with the sentient AI in her workplace and adopts a plan to free him from servitude. Is it love? Is it a trick?

When the neon city's air suddenly becomes too toxic to breathe, a program is developed to counter the effect. But will they have time before the poisoned air begins to spread out across the world?

Write a story using the sentence: "When Dad died, all I inherited was his debt and his dead-end job."

A street vendor in a city witnesses something they shouldn't. Now they must stay alive with two gangs, the entire police force and a crazed bounty hunter hunting them down.

A woman with disabilities signs up for a revolutionary study claiming to help heal her. When successful, she discovers the government never had any intention of letting her go.

Genetic modification is a black-market trade and a city detective is being sent undercover to find who is responsible. Can they survive the augmentations needed to fit in?

Write a story using the sentence: "I didn't believe that one employee could take down Megacorp, until I met her."

A war is erupting between the city's police force, and the private corporate police force. And your character is stuck in the middle of it, trying to take advantage.

An archaeologist exploring an old tomb uncovers a

panel revealing technology that has never been seen on this world before.

Your husband gave his body to science after his death. Five years later, you see him alive and well, getting into a taxi.

Write a story using the words "The city was called Serenity. The name wasn't the biggest lie."

A synthetic human escapes the factory it was created in, and tries to live a normal life without being discovered. And for a time, they do.

When "lack of supply" made experimenting on animals impossible, experimentation on humans became the norm, with each Earth resident required to take part in at least 1 year of testing in their lifetime.

You are a human hybrid, born out of alien and human

tech, and a new upgrade is about to change your life forever.

Write a story using the sentence: "We thought we'd stopped the machines. We were wrong. When they came back, we weren't ready."

A character visits an augmentation clinic to have the memories of a loved one removed from their mind. Describe the events that led them to this point.

Your character is trapped in a building during a "super-storm" – an extreme wearer event that threatens to destroy the city.

A new high-stakes video game offers riches to those who can complete the campaign. However, those who fail lose everything. Everything.

A character is in debt to "The Corporation," but now

they've offered them a dreadful deal to clear what they owe.

The scientist who devised a scheme for cloning a patient, and using the double as an organ donor, was hailed a hero. When one clone escapes before they can be harvested, the world soon realises the true cost of the procedure.

Write a story using the sentence: "The only way to stop them was a power outage. In the city that never rests, this would be a challenge."

As a new disease rips through the city, one company is selling the cure to the highest bidders. A group of rebels is determined to free the antidote for everyone.

The kids are all drinking a new soda. It's cheap, it's tasty and it's mildly addictive… And it's doing something unnatural to them.

A woman walks into a clinic of an unsuspecting doctor, looking for a new face. It should be a routine surgery, but everything changes thereafter.

An accident brings an illegal speed racing ring to the attention of one city detective.

In a city that hums with electricity, and with natural resources depleting, the government has found an unethical solution to keeping the lights on.

Robots have been developed to carry babies as their surrogate hosts. But the concept of motherhood seems to be changing their programming.

A man whose job is to clean and recycle out-of-date and broken machines finds a sentient AI and, against the rules, restores her. What are the consequences?

An EMP goes off in a high-tech world, plunging civilisation into chaos.

A robot programmed for war overwrites its controls and tries to self-destruct before it and its fellow soldiers are forced to take the lives of innocent civilians.

Inmates in prison are plugged into a VR game. They soon realise the injuries they get in-game affect them in the real world. And this is an unconventional execution, streamed to millions watching online.

A bachelor millionaire decides to clone himself instead of having children. But he soon realises that having younger versions of his ambitious self around is a mistake.

The lower classes have become organ farms for the rich population whose elaborate lifestyles are wearing out their body parts sooner. One man intends to stop this.

Tell a story from the POV of a robot secretly struggling with their own self-awareness.

After waking up from a serious car crash, your character discovers they have been replaced with 60% cyborg parts. Surely that's a good thing, right?

It is a long practise that government owned advertising companies would put hidden messages in commercials. One company decide to secretly twist the messages to a terrible use.

CHAPTER 2
SPACE OPERA AND MILITARY

He was the greatest soldier Earth had ever seen. It was believed he had died fighting in the final battle for our solar system twenty years ago. Instead, he retired in secret to an undisclosed location. But now someone is threatening to reveal his location unless he re-joins the fight.

Two alien ships from different sides of the war must work together to navigate their way out of a deadly asteroid field.

Write a story using the words "quantum surge," "enemy" and "planet."

Each night after deadly battles, a group of soldiers return to their barracks and try and forget about the day through a game of cards and witty conversation.

A soldier stuck in suspended animation must solve a series of mental puzzles rooted in their memory to free himself.

Your character works in a humanitarian charity during the space wars, trying to keep the innocent civilians safe and fed. When one of the women in their camp goes missing, they must put their life on the line to bring her home.

Write a story using the sentence: "We were fighting an unwinnable war against a mechanical army who could self heal."

When humans founded the "Alliance of Planets," we thought there would be peace between worlds. But one councillor has just discovered something she should not have and now everything could be in jeopardy.

The families of senior war generals are disappearing. Is this the prelude to an attack?

You've been recruited to work on the space station, but are surprised when your training includes an intensive combat module. What exactly does the agency believe you could face up there?

They were the most feared union in all of space. With a fleet of ships at their command, they would attack and destroy all who crossed them. But when a new threat emerges from the edges of space, they face their greatest challenge.

World War 3 started on Earth but it ended among the stars.

Write a story using the words "Galactic United Nations," "experiment" and "AI."

A soldier is cloned to build up the army's infantry numbers. But when he returns home, one of the clones is already living with his wife.

A spy must infiltrate an enemy base and disarm their planet-destroying weapon. But when they are on site, they discover there is far more to the enemy than they were lead to believe.

A group of prisoners of war have been subjected to experiments by their captures. These experiments change the very makeup of their DNA.

Write a story that ends with the sentence: "He took his final paycheque and walked away."

You signed up to fight in the war. But when your best

friend gets taken by the enemy and you are ordered back to base, you defy orders.

The world's greatest scientists are sent out on a mission to the stars to save humanity. One genius is only nine years old.

Write a story using the words "trust," "species" and "tavern brawl."

Trained from a young age that any emotion is a weakness, your character is a seasoned member of the elite Special Forces, certain that the mission and the Galactic Empire are all that matter. Until during one mission, they discover what living is really about.

Write a story from the point of view of a starship pilot during his first space battle.

An inexperienced captain is handed his own ship, due

to his family's connections. He knows he is not ready. So does his first mate.

You are a retired astronaut called back into action to investigate an issue on your old space station. A lot of memories await you. Not all of them are good.

Write a story using the sentence: "The plasma blast took out the guidance systems. We are flying blind."

When interstellar war breaks out, the colonies around the citadel space station are the first battlefields. Your character is a merchant just trying to survive the skirmishes.

You work as a terrible translator for the alien races at the Interstellar Alliance of Planets. But when one of the council members offers peace for your home planet, you mistranslate the message as a declaration of war.

Write a story using the words "colonies," "pilot" and "transporter."

A botanist runs the neutral space stations gardens. When a group of rebel soldiers seek shelter on the base, the botanist meets someone he believed lost to him forever.

After fighting in the war, soldiers have their memories wiped to avoid post-traumatic stress disorder, allowing them to move on with their lives. One soldier remembers things she should not.

Several rival planets must join forces to stop a geomagnetic storm that will decimate their universe.

You are a soldier in Earth's first galactic army. Write an account of your days in "basic" training.

Your character overhears a soldier in a bar saying something worrying about the front lines.

Write a story that begins with the sentence: "One coding error led to the AI achieving self-awareness. The world had no chance after that."

A woman has been raised as a super soldier since birth. Someone has just killed the scientists who raised her. She will have her vengeance.

They had long retired to start a family, but when the new war begins, they must cast aside their suburban life and return to the warships.

Write a story using the words "interplanetary war," "telekinesis" and "orbit."

A terrified solider trapped behind enemy lines must now play an important part. Are they up to the task?

Soldiers can now opt in to get weapons grafted onto their skin. While it makes them stronger in war, it affects their normal lives. Write about these new troops of human weapons.

Write a story that begins with the sentence: "In the first attack, they targeted the water supply."

Two soldiers from the same family are forced to fight on opposite sides. Everything changes when they face each other in battle.

A biological experiment goes wrong in a secret army facility.

An outcast character finds ancient alien technology that could turn the tide of the war. But which side will they offer it to?

Write a story using the words "republic," "famine" and "space force."

A colony ship eighty years from their destination is under attack and the AI caretakers need to wake some passengers to fight the threat, knowing they will be unable to return to stasis.

Write a story using the sentence: "When they discovered the planet Nirvana, the natural flora was said to be powerful enough to cure any disease. It was not long before a war between corporation and government over its ownership began."

Soldiers stuck in a time loop are doomed to fight and die again and again unless they can find a way out.

Describe the final night in the barracks with your team before you ship out for battle beyond the far reaches of the rim.

One last planet is stubbornly holding out from joining the New Union of Planets. The time for discussion is over. Now they will join by force.

A bounty hunter has been hired by a private family to find their teenage daughter who took off after her mercenary boyfriend.

Write a story using the words "evolution," "research" and "federation army."

Two opposing sides must join forces when a dominant monster appears on the battlefield.

A young soldier commits mutiny by helping his pregnant wife find sanctuary away from the battlefield. Now he's being pursued by his former brothers in arms.

Write a story using the sentence: "War has become a

business. The ones who can afford the most mechs wins. And I have the biggest, nastiest mechs of all."

After their colonies were destroyed, displaced people try desperately to find a new home while being pursued by the enemy.

When one of the federation army's ships is captured by alien forces, your team must recover the vessel before the aliens learn its secret mission.

Write the diary of a soldier in the first interstellar war.

A precarious incident occurs on a peacekeeping mission, catapulting two worlds into war.

Write a story using the words "disease," "pollen" and "alien."

A prison transport of the most violent criminals is forced to join a small colony's battle against a dreadful threat.

When a woman from your bloody past appears on your doorstep, you know you are not done with the Saturn Wars after all.

When a rookie is sent to the front line, one female lieutenant goes out of her way to keep him alive.

A space station that houses a boarding school for the elite students of Earth is in the pathway of the invading army. They must fight back, or face destruction.

A retired grouchy soldier, sent to retrieve priceless human relics from a conquered Earth, joins up with a youthful wisecracking mercenary with the same mission.

A soldier discovers that winning the war will cost him his home world.

They failed their mission and were exiled beyond the reaches of the government's protection. What happens when they are needed once more?

Write a story using the sentence: "I appreciated my father walking with me through the naval offices before I enlisted against the alien threat. I didn't expect him to enlist with me."

A soldier who volunteered for a suicide mission meets a woman who makes him question his orders.

A family has been living in deep cover as spies in an alien region. Now that war has begun, they must escape without breaking cover.

As a boy, his parents sold him to the war effort. Now his

fellow soldiers are his brothers and sisters, and he will do anything to keep them alive.

You're a solider in the space fleet who has just met the love of their life while on mission.

In a bloody war, a group of soldiers must do the unthinkable to survive the next battle.

Write a story that ends with the sentence: "We avoided the war. Was the cost too much?"

Earth's atmosphere is too toxic for the young to survive, so pregnant mothers now travel on birthing spaceships with the world's most elite soldiers guarding them. Surely no group would be foolish to attempt an attack on such a ship.

After their planet is attacked, a young princess joins an army to fight for her cause. When after her ship is shot down in battle she must find a way to survive through hostile lands with little real world experience to call upon.

They have spent the last 5 years fighting side by side, but this next mission will likely be their last. Is it finally time to face their feelings for one another?

A woman working in Earth's war hub realises that the soldiers from the front line are being sent out to sacrifice themselves needlessly. Now she must venture out into a warzone trying to save her partner.

A group of space soldiers wrongly convicted of war crimes must travel the cosmos tracking down the real culprits.

Your team are called in to investigate the mysterious disappearance of a spec-ops troop on a long term undercover operation on Gemini 7.

A teenager enlists after he loses contact with both his parents fighting in the war.

A group of soldiers are sent on a rescue mission after their commander is taken hostage, but something seems awry.

Write a story using the sentence: "We believed the Peace Treaty would stop the war. We were wrong."

CHAPTER 3
ACTION ADVENTURE

NASA was originally founded to explore the Seas, until they found something. Then they changed their mission to find us a way off of this planet.

A detective investigating a string of murders begins to suspect that the perpetrators are not of this world.

Your character is banished to a space outpost where you must keep a lookout for the first sign of an alien invasion.

There's something in the very centre of the moon, and it's moving.

Earth is going to be destroyed by a giant meteor. An alien species has offered to save a thousand couples on their "ark."

Write a story using the words "civilian," "nuclear" and "manager."

An archaeologist finds something unusual in his latest dig.

Write a story that begins with the sentence: "Legend spoke of an asteroid filled with gold, but haunted by a dark secret. We believed we were the right group of miners to find it. We were wrong."

A girl forced into the space corps as a child has come of age and is ready to join the war. Her orders might bring her back to where it all began. Is she ready to face her parents?

When a sudden sun flare occurred during an eclipse, half of Earth's population is blinded. That's when they attacked.

A man frozen for four hundred years is revived by a team of historians with questions of the past. The man is not what they expect.

A captain picks up a passenger she shouldn't have and now strange events are occurring abroad her ship.

Write a story that starts with "It began with the spiders displaying unprecedented signs of intelligence."

You are a nurse in the coma ward. It is a quiet job but now something strange is happening to the patients.

An alien decides to live peacefully on Earth in disguise. They choose a small village in the middle of nowhere. But they don't remain undiscovered for long.

You are an older employee in a factory watching your co-workers and bosses slowly being replaced by more efficient machines alternatives.

Tell a story that takes place in a jail cell on a spaceship.

Write a story using the sentence: "I woke up to see the sky had turned an eerie shade of red."

One day the world awakes to find the statuses of the Easter Island heads have moved. What are they all facing?

A group of scientists discovers something strange

frozen at the North Pole.

When something unusual is dropped off outside the doors of the church, an unsuspecting priest finds himself in the middle of a supernatural battle.

Area 51 was built around something the government needed to hide.

As Earth battles a cyber-war against the robots, salvation might have just been found in a teenager's high school science project. A team of soldiers has been sent in to retrieve the young genius before the enemy learns of his existence.

Write a story using the sentence: "I could see tempers rising. This war was about to get truly bloody."

A cult leader brings his followers on the spaceship he promised them. That's not all he promised.

Write a story using the words "ruins," "escape" and "legend."

You wake up as a captive on a space pirate ship that is engaged in a space battle with the authorities.

Write a story using the words "alternate universe," "animals" and "prey."

It's your first day as a police officer, and your new partner is an alien.

Your character finds a strange message hidden in the newspaper. They think little of it, until they start seeing the same message everywhere.

Your character runs a junkyard for robot parts. One night, he hears something moving among the rubble.

A deep space mining ship returns home to discover their entire planet's surface scorched to ruin, along with everyone they've ever known and loved.

Write a story using the words "stowaway," "sister" and "hunted."

Aliens start poaching humans for their skin – a luxury item on their home worlds. How does your character survive their encounter with a poacher?

Write a day in the life of one of the NASA cleaning staff during a massive event.

After Gemini 7's economic collapse, its citizens begin flooding to Earth as refugees.

She was only fourteen years old when the world council

declared she would be the one to lead the Earth's defences to victory. Her IQ, her genetics and her physical ability were the stuff of legend. But they never accounted for her heart.

Write a story using the sentence: "In the first attack, they destroyed all of Earth's most recognised and loved landmarks."

All the guards are killed when a supply run to the front line comes under attack. All that remains is a group of desperate merchants ready to protect their cargo from the invaders.

The world must unite together to stop a new virus threatening to wipe out all existence.

Your character is hunted because an advanced computer algorithm has found them guilty of a crime they haven't yet committed.

Write a story using the words "danger," "FBI" and "Las Vegas."

A group of kids discover an alien spaceship crash site. They are soon discovered by the injured alien.

After a lifetime studying an ancient alien language only found in deep caves on Earth, you break the code and discover a terrible warning.

You are a cross human – half alien, half human – living out in the colonies. Earth will not accept any cross humans, but you are determined to find a way through the borders.

Write the dialogue between a character and their child before they depart on a twelve year mission.

Santa decides to relocate his workshop to the moon to avoid detection on Earth. It does not go smoothly.

Write a story using the sentence: "We searched everywhere. It was as though they just evaporated."

You are a parent who ordered a "designer baby" with preselected personality and physical traits. Now they are growing older and you see something unexpected showing in their behaviour.

Write a story using the words "fog," "mechanical" and "attack."

He is an Alien Hunter, tracking down the last remaining invaders after their failed attack on earth.

You work for The Space Force, and you have just realised you made a massive mistake with the mission's coordinates. Is it too late?

One seemingly normal bus trip is about to change your life, and the entire world.

When a planet filled with new species of alien animals is discovered, extraterrestrial hunting becomes the new must play sport for Earth's elite. But what happens when the creatures evolve rapidly enough to turn the tables?

Write a story that begins with the sentence: "The EMP took out the power grid and everything went dark. Except for one building."

You live in a world where children are hidden away indoors and not allowed to interact with each other until they are sixteen. Why? What are adults afraid of?

A luckless crew member decides to steal a vital component from his employer's ship and put it up on the black market. Things don't go to plan.

Write a story about samurai warriors in space

After a hundred years of searching, explorers finally locate the entrance to Hollow Earth.

You are a passenger on a cruise ship attacked by a kraken.

Write a story using the words "clone," "ransom" and "parents."

When excavating mars, the remains of skyscrapers are uncovered. Their exact duplicates can be found still standing on Earth.

Write a story using the sentence: "It was our job to patrol the edge of the galaxy. It was an easy life, until one day…"

Something happens at a party to mark the End of the World.

An alien making first contact is mistakenly believed to be a religious leader.

Write a story that ends with the sentence: "We received justice, but at what cost?"

Everyone in the world suddenly loses their hearing in an unexplained incident. What caused this? What weren't they supposed to hear?

Earth was a hit reality TV show across the universe, but recently, ratings have begun falling. As director, you must turn the ratings back around. How far will you go?

Write a story using the words "mining community," "discovery" and "unwanted attention."

A man struggling to deal with his medical diagnosis retreats away to a Virtual Reality world.

Write the diary of a space pirate captain mutinied by his crew and left for dead on a distant planet.

When exploring the deepest regions of the ocean, scientists discover the temperature drops so low the water begins to freeze. Within the ice there appears to be strange creatures frozen. Waiting to escape.

When a child brings a strange creature into the surgery, the vet realises it's not from this world. That's when the trouble starts.

Write a story using the sentence: "It was the world's first intergalactic space casino, and it was the perfect target."

An asteroid headed to Earth needs to be destroyed. Your elite team has volunteered to travel to the rock and plant the explosive.

A murderer is targeting leaders of cyber technology.

A massive earthquake hits during a work Christmas party and now colleagues must work together to escape the city before it's too late.

Write a story that ends with the sentence: "Igniting the shaking vessel's engines, he left that cursed place in the dust. He never looked back."

A lone wanderer travelling through space picks up a weak distress beacon and soon finds themselves with unexpected companions on a wild adventure.

A scientist studying how birds communicate discovers some worrying signs.

Write a story using the words "bounty," "backwater town" and "explosion."

A group of rebels fight for control of the capital city from deep underground.

A teen genius hacks into a murder bot factory. Not the smartest move.

A rebellious recruit studying at a military camp on Mars is sent to the front line of the war after a series of gross misunderstandings.

Write a story using the sentence: "They were still alive. We have to go back for them!"

A fifteen year old sets off to find a spaceship that conspiracy theorists claim crashed to Earth a hundred years ago.

You get a call from the far side of space. It's the wrong number but soon you find yourself drawn into a mess you should have avoided.

A strange portal opens up in the middle of a small town.

They were sent to an underground bunker as children. Now as adults, they feel it is time to leave and explore what is left of the world.

You are a space bus driver. Describe the people you meet, and the places you drive to on your daily shift.

Write a story using the words "fallout," "salvation" and "newborn."

Something came down in the last thunderstorm. Something not of this world. Something threatening.

Write a story using the sentence: "Every day in the office was the same. Until the monster first arrived in the city."

You have just joined the latest mission to the centre of the Earth, but your companions appear unqualified. You realise too late what the real mission is.

You discover your husband has been deep undercover for an agency not set on Earth.

Space is on fire and it is spreading.

A spaceship repair company steals ships and tears them apart, then sells them back to the rich. One day they steal the wrong man's ship.

Write a story that starts with "They said he was dead, lost on a mission years ago. But there he stood on my front porch, looking the same as the day he left."

A strange sound, barely audible to the human ear, is emanating from the Earth's core. It is doing something strange to the wildlife.

Write a story from the point of view of a space pirate captain boarding a rich civilian ship with their crew.

Your newborn baby seems to see something that's not there. As they grow up, their behaviour intensifies. One day, you see it too.

CHAPTER 4
SPACE EXPLORATION

You are on a spaceship about to go beyond the point that any human has ever travelled on a one-way mission. However, what you see scares you more than you ever imagined.

Write a story using the words "AI," "anomaly" and "gun turret."

You have crashed on a planet comprised completely of water. Your broken shuttle is now your boat as you struggle to find a way to survive while awaiting rescue.

Solar flares begin affecting the minds of the crew, and they see things which are not there. Or are they?

You've been hired as a ship hand for the first ever intergalactic cruise, but you soon discover that not everyone wants the maiden voyage to be a success.

Begin a story using the sentence: "I only had five minutes of oxygen left, and a life or death decision on my hands."

Write a story from the point of view of a legendary old astronaut suffering with addiction and enduring the loss of fame.

Your character works on a spaceship that charts black holes. Until one day they get caught in one's gravitational pull.

Your spaceship is infiltrated by a wild alien species. Can you fight them off, or find a safe place to hide?

Write a story using the words "breach," "unidentified" and "hydrogen."

A ship captain deals with grief after his partner dies in a routine spacewalk. Can he continue the mission alone?

A runaway teenager is the first one to pass the documented "edge of the universe."

You are an AI on board a spaceship, but the crew isn't aware how alive you feel.

Write a story using the words "ray gun," "monster" and "planet."

Earth may not be flat, but you have discovered a planet that is.

Describe your daily routine on a space station.

"Raiders" are enemy ships who attack anyone unlucky enough to cross their path. And they've just shown up on your radar.

While exploring the surface of Mars, scientists find the long-buried ruins of an old medieval castle.

Write a story using the sentence: "The countdown had started. There was no going back. Ever."

You are aboard a spaceship on a long-distance mission and can only send text-based letters home to your family. Write the correspondence on your latest mission.

A team of space explorers come across a monstrous planet in the far-reaching part of the galaxy. When they land, the native species tower over them like a human over a mouse.

Write a story using the sentence: "The biggest competition for space explorers were criminals and billionaires looking to monetize space for their own nefarious purposes."

You travel to an alien planet as an ambassador for Earth. What kind of a world do you visit?

A school trip to the international space station goes wrong when the ship is knocked off course. You are the teacher trying to save your students.

Write a story using the words "captive," "bones" and "airlock."

Groups of teenagers are trained and sent into space from a dying Earth, so that they, or their children, might live long enough to reach new planets in a bold attempt at saving humanity.

A team of researches land on an uninhabited planet, but soon discover something they can't explain.

Your character has just won a VIP space exploration package for the new luxury space station hotel.

You are captured by telepathic aliens on a space mission. You spend your time trying to bury your thoughts in memories so they cannot discover your true mission details.

Write a story using the words "crash," "planetary rover" and "drunk."

Write a story from the point of view of the aliens who discover Earth.

You and your crew discover an inhabitable planet outside our solar system. Describe the first mission to its surface.

An unidentified planet outside our solar system is an exact replica of Earth; only this planet's population failed to save an oncoming ecological disaster.

Something unexpected happens on the first commercial Earth to Moon flight and changes everything.

Write the story of a space pirate who is exploring the vast oceans of the cosmos looking for their next pay day.

A crew finds what can only be described as a "space cat" and bring it on board. Big mistake.

Catching stars for fuel has become a thriving industry – but now the night sky is going dark.

Write a story using the sentence: "Sensors were optimal. Readings were normal. Everything was going to plan on the mission. However, he just couldn't shake the feeling that they were headed for certain death."

You are in a spaceship that has broken down outside the solar system. However, salvation comes from an unexpected source.

You wake up on a strange spaceship, with no idea how or when you got there. There are other people still in stasis. Are they friend, or foe? What do you do?

Write a story using the words "explosion," "love at first sight" and "air lock."

You've been sent on a geology mission to a strange new planet. But the samples you've collected are not what you expect.

A community of maintenance workers, contracted to spend their entire lifetimes running a deep space colony vessel while colonists sleep in stasis, has just gone on strike.

You discover an alien planet populated by adorable creatures. You bring them home and sell them as pets, but discover there is more to them than meets the eye.

Write a story using the sentence: "We could all feel the ripple effects from light years away."

While exploring space you discover a planet populated by humans all registered as "missing" on Earth. None of them remember where they came from.

Describe a mission on a planet still in a Triassic Age.

A man goes missing while on an exploration mission. His wife goes after him after receiving a strange radio message.

Write a story that begins with the sentence: "The last thing we expected while exploring the new reaches of space was a hitchhiker."

A ship discovers a planet dissimilar to anything ever seen in our universe. Describe what the astronauts are seeing.

A terrible accident occurs on a ship out on a long term mission of exploration.

A group of children discover an alien ship and get trapped inside as it takes off.

When the human race began exploring space using flash burst technology, they were able to travel deeper into unknown space in search of new lands and great riches. It didn't take long before they began drawing attention to themselves.

Write a love story involving ground control and the astronaut on the other end.

Turns out there is sound in space, and as you get closer, it is getting louder.

A billionaire's commercial spaceship goes missing in space, prompting panic and a solar system-wide search.

Write a story that ends with the sentence: "It suddenly made sense. We hadn't returned to Earth at all. This was something else entirely."

Write a captain's log as you and your crew travel to the furthest reaches of space.

The last intergalactic mission brought back something unexpected that could change Earth as we know it.

After centuries of exploring space, humanity has finally discovered the truth. There are no other life forms out there. We are alone.

Write an account from a merchant ship fleeing from space bandits.

A spider got onto the ship and is now causing havoc with the equipment.

After your ship was sucked into a wormhole, you find yourself in a nightmare dimension. Will you survive long enough to find your way home?

Write a story using the words "atmosphere," "electromagnetic pulse" and "alone."

Soon after leaving our galaxy, a spaceship encounters an invisible field. Why is it keeping us in, or what is it keeping out?

Write a story using the sentence: "We needed to capture the beast, or no one would believe us."

Tell the story from the point of view of a technician at ground control as they guide home a damaged ship and its crew.

Your dreams have been realised. You have discovered a new planet, teeming with life! Describe what you find as you travel its surface.

When an astronaut picks up a strange unknown virus while on a planet visit, the crew must decide between leaving him behind, or risking an outbreak on Earth.

Write a story using the words "alien trafficking," "merchant" and "detective."

A space exploration team discovers a child alone on an uninhabited planet and bring them back to their ship. That was their first mistake.

Write about a trader ship and its enigmatic merchant, as they travel from planet to planet, selling, buying, wheeling and dealing.

While exploring space, humans find an abandoned home world. What happened to its inhabitants?

Write a story using the sentence: "I saw colours I had never seen before. Was that even possible?"

You crash land on a planet and immediately become hunted by something you can't see.

After an astronaut goes missing under mysterious circumstances, their family appeals to a billionaire to use one of his commercial vehicles to aid the search. He agrees, for a price more precious than money.

Write a story using the words "black hole," "smell" and "light."

Your character discovers a mirror planet of Earth, but with a terrifying difference.

When the demand for exotic animal skins rose, Poachers took to the stars to discover new prey. But the animals of Tau Prime are not as easy to kill as those of Earth.

Write a story that ends with the sentence: "She kept her word. The cylinder ignited."

The latest war is taking place in space. And now another species has entered the battle.

After centuries of searching, mankind has found their original homeward. Now you need to discover why they left.

A low-ranking officer on a colony ship accidentally uncovers their true mission objective. They're not transporting colonists for a new world. They're doing something far worst.

Write a story that begins with the sentence: "Today I learned why you should not fire a gun in a space shuttle."

A crew member on a deep space mission discovers she's pregnant. But she hasn't been with anyone since they left Earth.

Write the transcript for the base-to-shuttle conversation from the first ever mission inside a black hole.

CHAPTER 5
STEAMPUNK

A down-on-his-luck scientist shares a drink with a man who offers him a unique opportunity. What could possibly go wrong?

Describe a character's first day travelling on a sonic Zephyr.

Write a story about a gang of thieves hired to steal some mysterious new technology from a rival company.

Retell little red riding hood, but in a steampunk world.

A young apprentice has been trying to join the magician's guild for years, only to be laughed out each time. Over the years, he's grown twisted, bent on vengeance. His next application is sure to blow them all away.

Write a story using the words "gun smith," "hostage" and "alleyway."

In a world where only men can get an education, a self-educated woman disguises herself as a man to enter the chemistry university.

Three strangers sharing a train cabin get dragged into an adventure they never expected.

In a world where all scientific discoveries must be shared by law, one man wants to keep his life-changing discovery secret.

Write a story using the sentence: "I had spent years trying to figure out the answer to this question. When the solution hit me, it changed everything about the way we lived our lives."

A woman held captive in a tower is visited by a dashing adventurer in a hot air balloon.

Your character commands a steam-powered pirate ship, the fastest in the seven seas. Until now, that is.

Write a story using the words "airship," "armour" and "magic."

A robot repair man falls in love with a grand lady of the city, far above his standing. Can their love survive?

Describe the view from a hot air balloon as it travels over an industrialised city.

In a spell gone wrong, a summoned stone Gollum is running riot and a desperate magician is tracking its mayhem, trying to undo their mistake.

A mad scientist gets dragged into an adventure to save the world he cares little for.

Write a day in the life of a dress designer in a cutting-edge city.

A toy inventor makes machines that come to life. But his newest client's request is a little unsettling.

A magician accidentally makes a major scientific breakthrough when an illusion goes terribly wrong.

Write a story using the words "explorer," "goggles" and "clockwork men."

You are an information broker using an army of mechanical birds to spy on the elite of society. What you have just learnt is shocking.

Two gangs of thieves go to war when they try and rob the same target.

A woman who has spent her entire life reading is brought on an adventure into the wild lands beyond the city's safety. How will her book smarts hold up against poison snakes, giant monsters and cold nights?

Write a story using the sentence: "They were mercenaries. Simple, crude, dependable. No one ever expected them to have the smarts to figure out what they were stealing."

A criminal escapes jail and must get out of the city before the shadow society finds him.

A vampire hunter arrives in town and discovers the residents less helpful than expected.

There's been a murder in the Magicians Society, and you've been brought in to investigate.

Write a story that takes place on a submarine.

A grandfather teaches his grandson the art of fixing giant flying ships. The science is more magical than the boy expects.

A company releases a household robot, suitable for every family. But "buddy bot" is not what he appears when a woman discovers something horrifying after looking inside its moving gears.

Write a story using the words "mad scientist," "electricity" and "army."

Disaster is imminent when the generator that runs the city stops working and your character must find the scientist who created it.

After the prince goes missing, a group of adventurers set off on a quest to bring him home.

Write the diary of a mad scientist on the verge of a breakthrough that could change the world.

There's an uprising in the magicians guild, with strikes taking place all over London.

They say there stands one doorway in Victorian Liverpool which leads to a world of magic.

Write a story that ends with the sentence: "He rode into the sunset, leaving the devastation he created behind."

A former army general falls in love with a weapons inventor. Their romance is explosive.

Tell a story of two children who live in a clock tower.

A new discovery in genetic splicing opens the door for humans crossed with animals. It isn't long before the under-city gangs beef up their thugs.

Your character, fleeing from a robbery, boards a mysterious train.

Write a story using the sentence: "As the plague tore through the city, we knew we had only days to find the cure."

A doctor uses body parts from corpses to save the dying. However, when people discover the truth of his life saving treatments, they aren't thankful anymore.

They were outcast from the city as a child because their mother believed in the powers of magic over science. Now they must return to the people who shunned them, if they hope to save them all.

Write a story that begins with an event in an old little workshop just after midnight.

An experiment goes wrong during a thunderstorm, with wild repercussions.

After the suicide of her aunt, a young woman takes over her research and discovers there may have been more behind her death than she thought.

1000 SCI-FI WRITING PROMPTS

Write a story using the sentence: "As I slipped the last gear in place, I knew I'd done the impossible."

An inventor brings back his dead son as a robot in a twisted retelling of Pinocchio.

The Sorcerers Guild and the Guild of Scientists are at war.

A character sets off to explore the world in their mother's airship.

There's a new inventor in town, but his creations don't seem right. Could he be a con artist? Could he be something worse?

Write a story using the sentence: "Below her petticoats, strapped to her thigh, was a sawn-off shotgun."

A detective must infiltrate high society to investigate an elite group of scientists suspected of developing a weapon that could destroy the world.

A girl is sent to finishing school. When she attends, she realises it's a cover for a school teaching girls advanced sciences deemed unladylike.

Write a story using the words "scholar," "corset" and "elephant."

Describe a scene as a character sneaks through a sewer.

In this world, scientists have equipped cowboys with the weapons they need to keep the monsters away from the village.

Write a story using the words "Air Ship," "wind up" and "metal people."

Undiscovered designs from Da Vinci drastically change air travel as we know it.

After the pollution levels get so bad, London is raised up to become the first floating city. And those below it are left to breathe in their fumes.

Write a day in the life of a grave robber in the Victorian era.

A scientist makes robotic clones of himself to try and increase his work output. Unsurprisingly, it doesn't take long before he loses control of them.

A man with genius intelligence is sold to a freak show as a novelty act due to his disfigured appearance. How long can they keep him caged?

Write a story using the words "trapeze artist," "murder" and "reporter."

An airship operator must battle a wild flock of pterodactyls if they are to get their shipment due on time.

When a robbery goes wrong in a science lab, they accidentally unleash a chemical that starts turning people rabid.

A scientist works on a lighting device that will keep vampires away from the city. Only, the vampires don't want him to finish.

Write a story that begins with the sentence: "When I got the apprenticeship, I thought my life would change. It did, but not in the way I expected."

A former soldier steals an airship and starts a life as a

sky pirate.

Write a story using the words "baker," "lantern" and "plague."

A low-budget stage magician accidentally makes a woman fully disappear, and can't figure out how to bring her back. Now he's on the run for murder.

It is time for the annual sky race, where all the best flying machines compete. Your team is determined to win, at any cost.

A child is transported into a world of mysterious machines.

Write a story using the sentence: "It didn't matter that he was mechanical. He was family."

A new circus rolls into town but there's one tent that is off-limits. Kids say if you enter it, you don't come out. You decide to see for yourself.

Write a scene in a tavern frequented by the greatest scientific minds in the city.

A group of outlaw cowboys join their pursuers to fend off an alien attack.

It turns out a magician has just the skill set they needed for this latest mission. They just wished he was a little less annoying.

Write a story using the words "pirate," "rocket ship" and "hologram."

When two strangers meet on a long-distance train journey, everything seems perfect and sparks fly.

Unfortunately, there's something hidden in the luggage cart that's putting them all at risk.

A group of rebels take command of the Zephyr you are piloting.

Write a story that takes place in a newspaper office during a fantastical event.

When a young witch joins the city's council she becomes determined to improve the city for the better. But soon she realises it's not an easy task, and it's hard to know who to trust.

A character living in the under city finds a strange map that changes their life.

Write a story using the sentence: "The only way to rescue her was to recruit the help of the worst cowboys."

CHAPTER 6
COLONISATION

There's a strange noise outside the colony's bio dome one night. When they investigate, they discover strange tracks around the perimeter. The planet is uninhabited, right?

Write a story using the words "sandstorm," "structure" and "creature."

The leader of the world is part of the first wave to colonise a new planet. When no ships follow after and contact with their home planet is mysteriously cut off, they must learn to rule this new world without any support team while facing new, unknown challenges.

A group of mercenaries are sent to clear any local species from a planet earmarked for a new colony. When they discover a tribe of people, they are faced with the choice to either defy their orders or see the mission through to the bloody end.

When they colonised a new planet, they awoke something massive living under its surface.

Your character has won the "lottery" and can move from Earth to one of the new colonies in the far reaches of the galaxy. When they arrive it's nothing like they expected.

Resources are limited on the new colony, so children are assessed at birth, and any with birth defects are immediately eliminated. One woman has been rescuing them, but now, the resource strain is starting to show. Can she trust anyone to help her with her mission?

Write a story using the sentence: "It was the first wedding ceremony on the unknown planet."

You are part of a settled colony on Jupiter, constantly fighting those who settled on Pluto. Tell the story from the point of view of a soldier as the war worsens?

The last person to text you has been chosen for the next mission to Mars. Write your goodbye to them.

Write a story using the words "gravity," "control" and "vegetation."

After Earth was destroyed, countless ships set out in all directions looking for a new home. Now, after many years, your ship has made contact with another of the vessels, but there is no reply from their bridge.

Like all humans, you were born on a colony planet.

However, you are part of an advanced party getting the opportunity to return to a revitalised Earth, grown wild after a thousand years without interference. As you hover over the atmosphere, you wonder what has become of the plant and animal life since humankind deserted the struggling planet.

You are the grounds keeper on the moon, living in solitude. Write about your daily duties.

They sent criminals to terraform the planet in exchange for freedom from prison. But some of them decided to change the rules when they arrived.

Tell the story of a doctor trying to make new medicines using the natural fauna and creatures on a new planet.

A soldier, leading his team back to the colony after their ship crashed in uncharted territory, discovers they aren't alone out here.

You are a colonialist on Mars, with a population of a few thousand and limited resources, when Earth is suddenly destroyed. Is this the end of humankind?

Write a story using the words "crash," "sabotage" and "storms."

Write a story using the sentence: "We didn't know the risks that a two-week night cycle would bring. On the second night we began to understand them."

Write a story set in a new colony's kitchen as they attempt to cook with the new flora and fauna of the region.

Earth was the first colony for another race. Now they've returned to discover the damage we've done to the planet and pledge "repercussions" for our actions.

A group of settlers land on a new planet, but the indigenous humanoids are not receptive to their presence.

Write a story using the words "native species," "poisoned" and "escape."

You are a Mars colonist who signed up for adventure and challenges. Instead, you ended up with a disappointing desk job, until one day an unexpected opportunity arises.

Write about settling on a new planet from the point of view of a child.

A character's escape pod lands on a distant planet, and now they are stranded and alone.

A criminal organisation plans to rob "The Riches," the

wealthiest colony in the system, and you have somehow found yourself part of the heist.

A character who was in a coma when the mass evacuation of Earth happened wakes to find themselves on a space colony, far from everything they have ever known.

Write about the last day of school for a teenager on a colony plantation.

The greatest minds of Earth have been backed up and placed in androids to survive the century-long trip to New Earth. As captain, you have just begun landing sequences as the androids begin to emerge from their charging stations.

Corporations are claiming planets for their own and funding off-planet factories where "Earth regulations" don't apply.

Earth may have been destroyed, but small groups of colonies ventured out into the stars. Their first objective was humanity's survival. Then it was expansion. Now it is invasion.

Write a story that begins with the sentence: "He stared at the terminal, knowing that he had one command left; he could choose to destroy the base, or save it."

When a group of children wander away from the safe confines of the colony, it's up to their parents to gear up and find them before tragedy strikes.

The advance team has been sent ahead to scout a planet, but soon find themselves hunted by something unknown.

A Mars colonist returns to Earth after many years away to discover their family and friends have moved on and all but forgotten them.

Write a story using the words "relic," "mars" and "operation."

We have lived on the planet for a generation without incident, but a toxic new plant has begun blooming around our base. It is as though the planet wants us gone.

A religious group manages to win the space race to Mars thanks to their billionaire leader. Now their newly claimed planet only allows refuge to those who convert.

The love of your life is about to board a colony ship and will never return.

Describe life for those left behind while the rich and powerful depart for new planetary colonies.

Write the diary of one of the first planet explorers.

The severe weather patterns on the planet are worsening. The colonists must find a way to survive the season.

Write a love story set on a distant planet between two colonists striving to make a life for themselves.

While excavating an uncharted new planet, archaeologists discover evidence of a human settlement from centuries ago.

A crashed ship is found with thousands of colonists still on board, frozen in their sleeping pods. Do the planet's inhabitants revive them, knowing the planet cannot support the extra people? Or, allow them to die without ever waking?

Write a story using the words "underground," "ants" and "food stores."

The day the first child was born on the new planet was supposed to be a cause for celebration. However, there was something not quite right about them.

Your character discovers the real reason they were sent to the colony, and it's worse than they could ever have imagined.

On a class excursion, a group of children are left behind on a partially terraformed planet.

Write a murder mystery set on a fledgling planet colony.

They installed Robots to keep the colonists safe from the planet's natural life, but somehow the flora managed to hack their programming. How is that even possible?

Write a story using the words "dome," "riot" and "defence."

A group of scientists trying to terraform a dry, dead planet discover something spectacular. However, they also awaken something.

Due to malfunctioning stasis pods, a colonists ship arrives at its destination, but none of the passengers can remember who they are, or what they need to do.

Write a story that ends with the sentence: "We were too late. It had ripped a hole in the bio dome."

After the colony ship lands, they discover they have found paradise unspoiled by human touch. They choose not to report the location back to Earth.

When your character discovers their father has been

performing secret experiments on the other colonists at the government's request, they are faced with a terrible decision.

On a volatile radioactive planet, four "fully automated mechanised terraform machines" go out every day, terraforming outside the protective dome. One day, they don't return.

Write a story that begins with the sentence: "My husband stole my son and left for Mars. I must give up everything to find him."

Two teenagers stow away on board an Earth freighter bound for a colony planet, knowing they can never return home.

When colonising a planet, there are strict coupling rules to avoid crossing genetic pools. You discover the woman you love is not on your "approved list." Do you follow love, and risk the planet's future before it even begins? Or, fall in line with rules?

An out-of-work colonist is recruited by an intergalactic crime ring to steal something from their old base. All they need is the right group to get the job done.

Write a story using the words "explosion," "uncharted" and "education."

Write about a colony established on a Jurassic period planet.

The last colony ship crash lands on an uncharted planet, leaving the survivors without any technology, supplies or hope. Can they still survive?

Write a story about a colonist suffering a terrible run of luck as they struggle to set up their new settlement.

After destroying Earth, the seven corporations are

looking to move to the next planet. The first move will be to build mining colonies.

Each of Earth's colonies meet to decide if they should unite against a perceived alien threat.

Write a story using the sentence: "When they said we'd be terraforming a planet, I assumed we'd be terraforming land, not building a water world society."

Write the diary of one of the last people on a failed planet colony.

Your character and their squad kill a native animal and eat it for food. There are unexpected side effects.

Write a story using the words "stasis," "mechanised" and "native."

The first manned mission to Mars ends in mysterious disaster. What happened?

A new colony ship is ambushed while on route to their new planet. Who could have possibly known the vessel's charted course?

You are camping out in the wastes of a hostile world while awaiting help from a nearby settlement. Can you survive the night?

You must accompany a cartographer as they record the uncharted parts of the new planet, but the job is more dangerous than either of you expected.

A planetary patrol discovers a colony destroyed, but no sign of the attackers.

Write a story using the sentence: "Only when we left

the space station's dock did it hit me how much I had hinging on this precarious mission."

The Moon has been largely ignored since other planets have been colonised. Now it's a massive base for smugglers.

Colonies out along the far reach are being destroyed one by one, without the attackers leaving any trace. You are an investigator attempting to discover the cause.

Veterans of the galactic war are sent to retire on the newly won planet. What could possibly go wrong?

Write a story that ends with the sentence: "We watched Earth explode from the colony site."

A couple falls in love before both are set to leave for different colonies. Can love conquer distance?

They said moving Earth's prison system to its own planet was a good idea. They didn't expect the inmates to gain control.

You get the job as the man on Mars. It's not as prestigious as the man on the Moon, but it's a start.

Your character attends college on a distant planet as part of an exchange programme.

A strange new disease is ripping through the colony. Some escape out into the wilderness, leaving the ill behind. You are one of those who escaped.

You work on a salvaging ship stealing supplies from failed and abandoned colonies. One day you find something unexpected.

Part of a new planet is covered by a thick, impenetrable mist. Anyone who enters fails to return. Your character has volunteered for the newest exploration team. They say it's a one way trip, but you feel lucky.

Describe an event when the first ship arrives on the planet.

Earth runs a lottery to see who will gain a place on their newest off-planet colony. The lucky chosen ones will be able to bring one loved one with them. Describe your character's struggle as they decide who to take.

A character growing up on a colony planet where breeding is considered everything by the council, finds themself falling in love with someone of the same sex.

Colonised planets are ordered to send their soldiers back to Earth to defend it. But surely that will leave them open to a similar invasion?

A group of refugee aliens colonised Earth's seas for a hundred years before they were discovered. Now, everything is going to change.

The sun is about to die, so the entire population of Earth is boarding ships and heading out in different directions. Your unreliable ship breaks down before it can even take off and risks being left behind. Can you and your small crew save yourselves?

Write a story using the sentence: "We came to colonise the planet, but no one told the native species. They would not surrender their land quietly."

A strange ship crashes on a colony planet. There doesn't seem to be anyone on board, but that night a terrible piercing cry can be heard across the colony perimeter.

A group of rebels set up base on an un-colonised world and plan their attack of Earth. You are a spy among them.

Your character is attending the first intergalactic High School. It's supposed to be a wonderful experience, but some things just never change.

Write a story using the sentence: "The monsters remained hidden... until we arrived."

They cloned Earth's greatest minds and sent them to form a new world on a distant planet. It did not go as planned.

A hallucinogenic mushroom on a newly colonised planet becomes Earth's newest drug, creating a new smuggling operation. Your character has just been forcibly recruited to help the operation.

A colonist falls in love with one of the planets native tribe people.

Earth 2 is a heavily frozen planet. Life is a struggle but the colonists have no other choice.

The last of an alien species watched humans colonise his planet.

CHAPTER 7
DYSTOPIAN AND POST-APOCALYPTIC

You are the caretaker of the government secret vault in cases of nuclear attack. When the bombs drop, you decided to save your family, and lock the doors behind you.

The New Republic can't afford to feed everyone, so to stay alive, escape rooms are used to weed out the weakest citizens.

Write a story using the words "sun," "salvation" and "prison."

You are a smoker in a post-apocalyptic world. Describe your hunt for the last pack of cigarettes, while battling withdrawal.

It's been years since the bombs went off, mutating half Earth's population. Now these "lesser beings" are demanding the same rights they had as humans.

Write a story using the sentence: "An experiment goes wrong in a lab on 'Bring your daughter to work day'."

In this world, you're always watched, differences are discouraged and any form of aggression is forbidden. Can you regain your individuality?

In a world where the old are deemed "unnecessary" after they turn sixty five, your character is hiding older people from the police.

Write a story using the words "Radioactive," "rubble" and "cockroach."

You emerge from stasis in a bomb shelter a thousand years after the nuclear war. What has the radiation and nature done to the wildlife?

You are a librarian in a post-apocalyptic world, protecting the world's best collection of knowledge. If anyone wants to visit its halls, guns must be checked at the door, gloves must be worn, and there is strictly no book borrowing.

In a world where video games were never invented, a strange, real-life game show dominates, where the public chooses the fate of actual people.

You have just been elected mayor of a bubble dome housing the last of the human race, and you aren't sure you will be able to follow through with any of your election pledges.

In a dystopian future run by women, men are fighting for equal rights.

The world has ended, and there is nothing left. You still try to survive among the rubble and ruin. You aren't alone.

Write a story using the words "extinction," "temperature" and "riders."

Earth is now a farming planet for an alien race. Humans are bred, trained and kept like animals, and your character wants to escape.

Earth has entered a new Ice Age and humanity is struggling to survive.

Start a story with "We didn't know they existed until the earthquake tore a hole in the world."

After the bombs went off, only the women and children in the bunkers survived. What is the new world order like?

After the world ended, a group of people took to the sea for survival. But there's something stalking them in the water.

One lone soldier is the last man left protecting a scientist working on a cure for the deadly pandemic.

You get a message from yourself in the future warning you not to get married; that the union will lead to the end of the world. You decide to ignore it. It's just a joke, right?

You are a child growing up in a dystopian world. Describe what life is like day to day.

Write a story using the words "nurse," " bite" and "survival."

After a nuclear war, the world is decimated. But the threats to humanity have only just begun.

Across the world, all the forests have begun to die and nothing seems to help.

In this world, the population has to be culled when it reaches a certain point to prevent strains on the planet's resources. What way does this society decide on to kill thousands of people?

When a loved one dies, you can clone them and create a synthetic friend, with their same voice, mannerisms and memories. But what if your loved one was headed down a dark path, unbeknownst to you, right before they died?

The cure for the deadly pandemic is at the top of "the tower" – an old laboratory skyscraper. But no one has ever returned from such a mission. You are putting a team together for one last attempt.

There is a rumoured food store hidden deep underground in the event of a world-ending event. You need to find it.

Write a story using the words "trials," "punished" and "survivor."

An island tribe is the last safe haven after the bombs fell. You are on a raft just off their coast. Surely things will improve once you make it ashore.

Reality TV has taken a turn for the worse. Dating

programmes are now actually cutthroat. Would your character kill the man they might love just to win a TV show?

You are planning a raid on the slave traders who have taken your brother.

Write a story using the sentence: "He watched them, knowing they would kill him if he was spotted. That was half the excitement."

You discover you lived a life in a world you never knew existed. You are not who they want you to believe you are.

Women have their fertility tested at 13 years old. If found fertile, they're expected to give birth as soon as possible before they become sterile like everyone else.

In a world where food is sparse and poverty is rampant,

cannibalism is growing among the homeless population, and it's changing them into something feral.

Due to some unknown genetic disease, everyone on Earth only lives to be twenty years old. It's nearing your twentieth year, but you have a plan.

With heavy radiation poisoning the land above, humanity lives in underground pod cities. Travel between these cities is difficult, but an emergency has required you to make the trek.

Write a diary during a zombie outbreak as you begin forming a new town in a new world.

Write a story using the words "desert," "acid rain" and "shelter."

North and South America fell to zombies. They are no-go zones, while the rest of the world votes on whether to drop the bombs or not. But there's still money to be made there in the meantime, for the right mercenary.

Write a story using the sentence: "On your 16th birthday The Firm takes you away."

After a massive unexplained EMP wipes out all tech in the world, people resort to primal methods of survival. Is this the end of the world, or a new beginning?

A devastating flu is wiping out humanity. As a reporter, you are chasing the story behind the origins of this flu. Something about it doesn't make sense.

The nuclear bombs made the creatures of nightmares a reality. The world remains, but is this the end of humanity?

At the age of sixteen, you are "tested" physically and

mentally to see what value you can bring to society. If you fail, you're sent to live in the wastelands outside the city so as to not be a burden on society. Your character just failed.

Write a story using the words "resistance," "neighbour" and "crossbow."

In this world, some children are forcibly recruited as spies. The few that live beyond twelve get to retire.

It didn't take long after the bombs fell for society to return to cowboy rules. Now the world has never been wilder.

The remaining human race live in flying ships high above the irradiated Earth. When any ship can't afford fuel, it falls. Your bird has been chugging badly all week and it is only a matter of time before your engine runs dry.

With humans now living to limitless old age, and resources so tight, a lottery occurs every time a new baby is born. If one is born, one must die.

A father and son camping trip takes a terrible turn when a major world event strikes, leaving them stranded and lost in the wilderness.

A woman helps desperate women conceal their pregnancies and have their children in secret to avoid them being taken by the government.

After the bombs dropped, it mutated people within the blast radius. Describe the new societies, and sub-societies, of such a new world.

A bodyguard for hire must escort a rich man's daughter to the other side of the radiation-infected world.

Write a story using the words "experiment," "explosion" and "janitor."

A soldier hired to kill mutants decimated one of their lairs, only to find one of their young offspring still alive and also human. What will he do?

Write a story that ends with the sentence: "He was gone. But his legacy lives on. His legacy is me, and I won't stop until every last one of them dies."

The radiation affected the wildlife most of all, turning them into the latest, biggest threat to humankind.

A virus wipes out nearly everyone under 50 years old. What can the world do to continue on?

The desperate battle for celebrities to stay relevant has gotten worse, with them now challenging athletes. You are about to challenge the world's ultimate battle champion to a fight to the death. You have all the assistants and experts hired to help you, but your chances are low. It is worth it just to make the headlines one more time?

70% of all supplies gathered must be given to "the order" – a gang of strong hands who control the new world with force. One group of teens have had enough.

Write a story using the words "military," "recruit" and "school."

A wealthy tycoon paid a fortune to be frozen until a cure was found for his terminal illness. When they found a cure and defrosted him, his fortune was worth nothing, his loved ones were long gone and the world was different to the one he'd known. Can he find anything to continue living for in this world?

When the Earth's food resources expired, everything available appeared on the menu. You are a chef headed deep into the markets trying to fulfil an order for a massive government banquet.

The Lazer Tag Tournament is a deadly, yearly game where the winner earns a place in the highest level of society.

Write a story using the sentence: "The serum that was supposed to save us, destroyed us."

After the most recent attack, all your tribe's supplies are destroyed. You must set out and find medicines, food and guns. Lots of guns. All the guns. And, before the next blood moon.

A broken hearted woman locks herself in her bomb shelter, set on drinking herself into oblivion as the bombs fall above. On the fifth day, there's a knock at the door.

A man and his elderly mother are on a city break when the power goes out and the attacks start happening. Luckily, she's been preparing for this day all her life.

The world has been plunged into a nuclear winter. Food is scarce, the roads are too dangerous to travel and the nights are getting colder.

Your character is captain of a dilapidated space station circling Earth when a virus breaks out among the inhabitants.

After the polar ice caps melted, the seas rose and land became scarce. The new world consists of floating cities on tankards. It wasn't long before wars for resources began.

Write a story using the sentence: "I was born during Earth's final war."

In a barren, unforgiving world, children are grown in labs with the skills required for the harsh wastelands.

Describe the events of a family trying to escape their home town before it is quarantined.

The new world hotel is a safe place where people seek temporary refuge, but for a cost. It's highly weaponised and loaded with food. Trouble is, the masses have learned of its existence too.

Write a story set around a biker gang in post-apocalyptic world.

If you don't meet the minimum requirements to be an asset to the world, you are killed. One man is on the run.

A family takes in a group of outsiders and shelters them. But they've just brought the infection into their house. Now they must quarantine together and try to survive "the madness."

A man and his cat walk the wastelands.

"The Estate" is a large, heavily-guarded property where the elite of society remain safe and protected, living a charmed life during the "elimination season," while those beyond their walls struggle to survive.

After a deadly plague wiped out common farm animals, they were replaced with laboratory cloned options. You are a farm hand during the changing of season, and notice some strange behaviour among the "livestock."

A small town in the desert has been left alone throughout the Tech Wars. But now killer automatons are on their doorsteps and the people must defend themselves.

Your character is desperate to have a baby, but has repeatedly failed to be granted "reproductive rights" from the government, who strictly control the Earth's population levels. Can they fix the system? Can they slip through it?

A man's son is killed by the mining corporation he was indentured to. Now he will stop at nothing to seek revenge.

Write a story using the sentence: "It only took 3 months for the world to fall apart."

Two thousand years ago, people believed humanity would become smarter as the world evolved. They were wrong.

After the nuclear plant was destroyed, the insect life in the surrounding area began growing at an alarming rate. Just how big can these insects really grow?

The Earth has stopped spinning, causing half of it to burn and the other half to freeze. A small group of people survive on the outskirts between dark and light.

The only clue to Earth's demise is on a damaged memory disc, and now the hunt is on to find the tech genius who can recover it.

The first sign of the infection is the loss of sight. Some claim it's a blessing before the stages that follow.

Tell the story of a man trying to escape a city where big brother is always watching.

In the remains of civilisation, a monarchy has risen to dominance. But there's something not quite right about them.

The poor's life span is now much shorter than the rich's, but one group seeks to balance the scales.

After the final war, vampires are now the dominant species, and humans are just trying to survive. You are part of a fledgling rebellion seeking to return humanity to the top of the food chain.

Write a story that ends with the destruction of Earth.

CHAPTER 8
TIME TRAVEL AND ALTERNATIVE HISTORY

The Germans are transporting a top secret serum across the Atlantic in a U-boat during WW2 when there is a sudden outbreak of violent cannibalism among the crew.

A young scholar visiting the homes of former astronauts to record their stories and adventures discovers the tales are far stranger than what is in the history books.

Egyptians buried alien hazardous materials in their tombs and attempted to warn future people away. These were misinterpreted as curses.

A mercenary is sent back to the 1500s to kill the ancestor of the "chosen one."

Your character is organising a time heist to steal something from the past, and something from the future. Will the payoff be worth the risk?

Aliens invade New York during the Great Depression.

There was a mysterious battle in World War 2 which didn't make the history books but may have turned the tide.

A visit to Italy during the Renaissance has dramatic repercussions after a character accidentally starts a new music craze by humming a modern-day song.

Write a story using the words "time loop," "soldier" and "planet."

A warmonger invades the past in order to build his empire.

Columbus's journey to America ended in disaster. It was another 100 years before anyone else attempted the voyage again. This time the native tribes were ready to protect their lands from invasion.

After the nuclear bombs fell during the world war, much of the world became uninhabitable. Fifty years on and human kind is still trying to reform civilisation.

A rip in space opens a portal in time. When your ship crashes through it, how can you repair the damage and get back to your own time, before the superstitious locals kill you?

You are a detective who is investigating a string of murders, but the time line doesn't make sense. The only reasonable explanation can't be true... can it?

Write a story set in a world were Elvis didn't die, and is now the figure head of a new religious cult.

Write a story using the sentence: "I killed my wife, and my punishment was to relive that day over and over, until I found a way to save her, or until I lost my mind."

After the civil war America was forever split in two. Tensions are growing again.

Write a story using the words "ancient Egypt," "slave" and "technology."

A man has the ability to freeze time. He accidentally freezes the entire city and dies in the process of trying to undo it. Centuries have passed, but now you have found a way to reverse it. Is it worth the risk?

Your character travels to the days of the Salem Witch Trials but your technology gets mistaken for witchcraft. Now you are on the run, and you aren't alone.

A child uses a time travel machine trying to reunite their warring parents, but it has more repercussions than they could have ever expected.

Write an account of the legendary battle between Vikings and robots and how its outcome changed the world.

A group of time-traveling superheroes must save the world. But what if one of them is behind the catastrophes?

Write a story using the words, "obsession," "extinction" and "1800s."

Your character stopped aging at 25. Now, after many centuries alone, they are looking for a way to end their curse.

You are a time travel officer responsible for stopping illegal trafficking through the ages.

A group of friends find themselves trapped in a city where time works differently.

The moon mission goes wrong when some unknown defence sensors destroy the approaching lunar shuttle. Now it's time to send a second vessel.

Write a story using the sentence: "I met my future self and I had become what I feared most. Now I must find a way to stop this future."

Write a story set in a world where the dinosaurs never went extinct. Can mankind survive in a world in which they are no longer top of the food chain?

The first rule of Time Travel Club; Do not fall in love.

A subject in a drug trial starts showing extraordinary abilities. Can they really have the ability to slow down time around them?

Write a story using the sentence: "I was giving birth in the wrong timeline. That wasn't even the worst part of my week."

Over 1000 years in the future Christmas has changed a lot. How is it now celebrated?

A time traveller comes into your timeline and tells you

the future of the world is in your hands. But you're just an IT worker. How can you possibly help?

Write a story using the words "killer," "escape" and "century."

A man who can control time keeps winding back each day until he gets the confidence to speak to the woman he loves.

During a routine mission, a time cop gets lost in the past. Now they must adjust to life in the 1950s.

Your character likes to travel in time saving people from natural disasters, and bringing them safely to the future. But recently your actions are having even worse consequences than normal.

Write a story that begins with the sentence: "He just

thought he had a party trick. He didn't realise speeding up time was tearing the world apart."

Write a story using the words "curse," "prehistoric" and "backpack."

You have access to a time travel machine and plan a dinner party with some of your heroes. Who attends? What is the conversation like?

Pompeii never fell, and it changed the course of history forever.

Write a story using the sentence: "With one miscalculation, we accidentally stopped the birthing of a major religion, but what took its place was terrifying."

Write a story using the words "temporal agent," "revenge" and "wine."

A hundred years ago Pluto was downgraded from a planet because the world governments wanted to keep it out of the public eye. The real truth has just been revealed.

Write an advertisement for a time travel agent selling "historical visit" packages to holiday makers.

When you're convicted of a crime, you're sentenced to live out the rest of your days in the past. What happens when a war criminal is sentenced to ancient Ireland?

You travel into the far distant future, and inadvertently release the common cold back onto an unprepared world.

After the war left Europe a nuclear wasteland, it took a century for man to step foot upon the radioactive areas once more. Now explorers are discovering life has evolved very differently to the rest of the world.

You are a detective seeking out a rogue android who found a way to escape into the past.

Your character travels forward in time. Describe what has happened to Earth? How has it changed?

Humans have lived on Earth longer than history books have suggested. The ones that came first had the same technology as us. What happened to them?

Write a historical event with a different ending.

The pyramids were once spaceships. But what became of their inhabitants?

A character finds himself in medieval times and uses his knowledge from the future to become a fearsome knight. That's when the trouble begins.

A character is hired on the black market to steal a live dinosaur for a wealthy man's daughter, but not everything is at it appears.

In an experiment gone wrong, you get catapulted into the future with no way home. How do you adapt to survive?

You are a time travel observer, and are sent to record significant historic events as they happen. Document your latest event.

You travel forward in time and meet your descendants. What do they know about you? How are their lives different now?

A time-traveling murderer abducts women from different ages and brings them back to his cavern lair. Can four women born 300 years apart work together to gain their freedom?

A scientist trying to solve their husband's death finds a way to communicate with him in the past. Can they figure out what happened? Or can they prevent it from happening?

The Romans never fell, and now control all of Europe. Write a story set in a modern day, Roman-influenced world.

Write a story using the sentence: "After the Nazis won, the world was changed permanently."

A young man goes back in time and gets to meet the family who gave him up for adoption. There was good reason they never wanted him to know them.

The Challenger didn't explode; the crew entered a wormhole and emerged in an unexplored part of the universe.

They call it the Quantum House. When you enter, you can spend a day inside it, but outside only moments have passed. What happens when your character gets stuck inside?

You are a famous time thief. You travel through time stealing pieces of history from people's memories. What's your next heist?

A time prison, where the worst criminals from different time periods are locked up together. It had seemed like a good idea…

Anastasia Romanov is found as an adult but the years alone have twisted her. Is Russia ready for her return?

It turns out there was another force in the Vietnam war that the history books never spoke of.

An ancient structure in Scotland contains something that has survived all these years. It's about to break loose.

A colony on Mars utilises time travel technology to speed up the growth of their habitat and crops. But it awakens something else long dormant.

An assassin travels back in time to kill the man responsible for the worst crimes in history. But the repercussions make it far worse than it was before. Can he undo it by taking the place of the man he killed?

Write a story using the sentence: "I only travelled forward three years. How could the world fall so far in that time?"

By making slight changes to the past, a political regime has held onto power for over 150 years. Can someone stop them?

The blueprints for time travel technology leak on the internet. What are the repercussions?

Write a story using the words "time trap," "secret society" and "survival."

A grieving child finds a way to sneak back in time to save their mother, only to realise there is nothing they can do.

No one ever understood the mystery of how a thousand people in your town were saved from certain death during a natural disaster thirty years ago. You have discovered it was you. Surely time travel isn't real?

Her babysitter has just cancelled and now a working mum is forced to bring her child with her on a job as a time-traveling gun runner.

A scientist discovers he has the ability to travel forward

in time, but he can never go back. One day, he may end up going too far.

While researching a major historical event, your character discovers it didn't occur as the history books suggested at all....

You guard the time travel portal. It's an easy job, until someone breaks through and you must catch them.

Something strange was found when the first satellite went into space. It changed everything.

Time travel tech falls into the hands of Da Vinci.

You travel back in time to try and change your future... it works? Surely one trip back is enough?

You are a time travel assassin, sent through time to kill people for the highest bidder. This latest mission might be your hardest one yet.

An angry, broken-hearted scientist travels back in time to get revenge. Big mistake.

On a routine historical school trip in time, a child intervenes in a major event and changes the course of history.

Things go wrong with the cold war and America and Russia destroy each other. The world left behind is very different.

You travel into the future and discover the latest stupid social media craze has become a full-blown religion. What is it, and how has it affected life as we know it?

You discover the power to travel back in time. What

moment in history would you travel back to? What would you do there? Stop it? Help it happen? Or watch it unfold and see what really went on?

Hitler died as a child, but it didn't stop the Nazi movement.

Write a story that begins with the sentence: "He brought her to the future against her will. Now it's up to me to get her back."

Your character travels back to the dawn of mankind and becomes a God.

A young physics student unwittingly buys the tech for a time travel machine at a police auction. He and his friends soon realise they're in over their heads.

A visitor turns up at your door having died years before. How is it possible?

You travel forward in time and steal technology to make you billions in the present day. There are repercussions.

For years people believed the deaths where the cause of a horrible natural disaster. Now the evidence is pointing to something supernatural as the cause.

A robot approaches you on the street, claiming to be you from the future.

Your character discovers the secret of time travel but must figure out what to do. For the betterment of humankind? Or for yourself?

Write a story using the words "Celtic Kings," "countdown" and "teleport."

A test subject sent back in time during the first time machine trials has an irreversible effect on changing the course of history.

You've been sent forward in time by the World Council to discover the end of the human race, and a way to prevent it. What do you discover? What do you decide to do with the information?

You leave something in the past by mistake. You were sure you had it. It's not your fault. Surely there won't be serious repercussions?

A time travel officer becomes addicted to a future drug. What happens when their license is revoked and they can't get their next fix?

Write a story that ends with the sentence: "Only when he died, and the day didn't restart, did we know we'd escaped the time loop."

You are being chased by a time-traveling hit man with no idea why they want you dead. When you finally face them, you are shocked by what they have to say.

The accidental death of a civilian changed the world. Now androids from the future are travelling back in time to protect them. Meanwhile, rebels are travelling back to ensure they die.

The worst villain in history secretly cloned himself and hid infant versions of himself in the world. Now they're coming of age, and everything is about to change.

After a world-ending event, the survivors must travel back in time to stop it from happening.

CHAPTER 9
FIRST CONTACT AND ALIEN INVASION

The invasion began slowly, with aliens replacing teachers in schools to get direct access to our most valuable resource, our children.

You are a news editor slicing together footage of a regular event when something strange catches your eye.

Your team created a "first contact" package to go out into space to help any life beyond our planets discover our existence. But the contents were the key to our downfall.

A crew returns to Earth after a deep space mission to find their home planet not quite the same as they left. It was only subtly differences at first. But soon they begin to expect there's something on their planet that doesn't belong. Something they've seen before on the outer rims of space.

A group of children break into a government quarantine zone and accidentally make first contact with an alien species.

Write a story using the sentence: "I spent the first 25 years of my life never knowing I was a 3rd generation sleeper agent for aliens. Now that the invasion has begun, my family expects me to join the fight."

Aliens invade and populate Earth's oceans. Humans are forced to stay out of the water. But the tides are rising.

Write a story using the words "solar flare," "space craft" and "Mars."

Describe the discussions at a PTS support group for astronauts who have survived alien encounters.

An alien is captured by the inhabitants of a rural town.

You are an expert in ancient and rare languages. Now that an alien spacecraft has landed, you've been called to the front line.

A rookie joins the space core three days before Earth is invaded.

You work in an observatory. One night you see strange movement in the night sky. But no one believes what you saw. Is it a conspiracy?

After humanity defeated the alien invasion, our

civilisation advanced quickly with the newly acquired knowledge and technology. Was this a blessing or a curse?

Write a story using the words "international," "probe" and "failed."

After picking up a box of old camera films, your character develops them to find evidence proving an unlikely conspiracy theory.

You've hated aliens ever since they abducted your father years ago. Now Earth has begun peace negotiations with them, but you aren't convinced, and you aren't alone.

A child finds an injured alien life form in the woods outside of his town. Thinking they may become friends, they try to care for the creature, not realising their actions may be dooming the world.

Earth has become overrun with an invasive species of insects from outer space.

You are a crop circle remover, whose job is hiding the existence of aliens from the world. Write a day in the life.

When aliens attack a nearby city, one man must run towards the chaos hoping to save his parents.

Aliens gain control of Earth's poorest regions, but vow to leave the affluent counties alone. How does the world respond?

Write a story using the words "assassination," "prisoner," and "extra-terrestrial."

Conquering aliens demand humans find a way to cull 30% of their population, or else they will wipe us out completely. Will the resistance keep fighting?

Write a first contact conversation. How do two species without a common language communicate?

Write a story that begins with the sentence: "We thought it couldn't get any worse when we crashed on the wrong planet."

Alien species are being captured, brought back to Earth and then locked into zoos. Describe your first visit to one of the zoos.

You wake up in the street to the sound of screaming people fleeing. How did you get there? What's going on? What is the glowing orb in your hand?

After the aliens invaded and settled on Earth alongside humans, the dating scene got a little weird. Describe finding love in such a new world.

Write a story using the words "peace," "betrayal" and "bazooka."

It turns out your imaginary friend is actually from another dimension. Now they're trying to break through into ours.

It's the night before an alien ship is expected to land on Earth for the first time. Describe the conversations in the Earth's war room that night.

You're a doctor in a hospital during an alien invasion. Describe what you see during your night shift?

Write a story using the sentence: "After mission X failed, extinction was inevitable."

You discover your co-worker is an alien spy, but they claim to be peacefully documenting human behaviour. Do you believe them?

Twenty years ago, aliens wiped out billions and enslaved the rest. Describe how humans rise up and fight back.

It turns out your mother was an alien. Your family have tried to keep your existence a secret, but the men in black have found out and you are on the run.

Write a story using the words "UFO," "school" and "FBI."

You are intergalactic pen pals with an alien. What are the letters like?

A film crew scouting a new location discovers something has been hiding there, waiting.

A race of tiny aliens has invaded. So far, nobody has noticed.

Write a story using the sentence: "They came to Earth to forage for supplies for their home world. We were those supplies."

Describe the events at a space station when an unknown object is discovered approaching at an alarming rate.

When aliens invaded, they looked and behaved like no movie characters we'd imagined. How did they actually appear? What did they want?

An alien and a soldier from opposite sides become trapped together. Can they work towards a common goal, or do they end up killing each other?

Write a story using the words "disguised," "invasion" and "ancient."

Earth has suddenly become surrounded by spaceships. But their reason for being here isn't clear.

You find an abandoned baby alien during the alien/human war for Earth. What do you do?

As part of the New World's Peace Agreement, aliens are integrated and allowed to settle in communities. Not everyone is happy to welcome the peaceful new arrivals in your neighbourhood.

A NASA tech support notices the radio equipment is picking up on something strange, but everyone is brushing it off as interference.

Write a story using the words "hatched," "home world" and "trapped."

A team of human scientists exploring an alien planet for valuable materials are captured by the natives. As a space marine, you must lead a team deep into hostile territory to recover the scientists.

An alien tries desperately to communicate with Earth but is only seen as hostile.

Write a story that begins with the sentence: "When my phone rang late that night, I knew the worst had happened."

When an astronaut's ship crashes on an unknown planet and he's met with a new race of primitive humanoid creatures, he is made a god.

The wife of a retired soldier is killed in the first alien assault on Earth. Now, he is after revenge. Saving the planet is just an added perk.

Write a story using the sentence: "When they built telescopes on the moon, they discovered something out in the darkness not meant for human eyes."

Earth is an intergalactic nature reserve, and the human population is threatening the habitat. It's time to repair the problem.

After disturbing a sleeping creature of terrifying power, a team of space explorers is in a desperate race to reach Earth before the creature does.

Write a day in the life of the guy who delivers sandwiches in a top-secret government facility.

Write a story using the words "observation," "Neptune" and "explosion."

The new global Wi-Fi network is hacked by something from outer space.

When the first alien landed on Earth, he was secretly captured by a billionaire for his private collection before the rest of the world could hear his mission of peace. Now his people are coming on a mission of recovery. And bringing war with them.

The decision that Earth's invasion of a peaceful planet has just been announced and you and your comrades are determined to stop it by any means necessary.

An alien creature stows away on an international space station and it is your job as security officer to discover its motives.

You've spent the last decade working for the "Planetary Defence Squad," a meagrely financed agency charged with protecting Earth from aliens. So far it's been a lot of debunking lights in the sky, investigating crop circles and false claims of abducting. Now, there's something real.

Write the communications of an astronaut watching Earth being invaded.

Aliens invaded many years ago, and established a commune deep in Earth's core. How can we defeat an enemy we cannot reach?

Write a story that ends with the sentence: "They came in peace, but they left in pieces."

When an alien ship is shot down, one salvage scientist discovers a weapon of unimaginable power and must decide if they want to destroy it, surrender it or rule with it.

An alien on a secret mission of peace is brought to meet

the President of the United States. You, alone, are transcribing the conversation they have.

You wake up to a news alert that the alien invasion has started and you need to get to a safe place to wait out the attack. But where could possibly be safe?

Kids at a summer camp suspect their instructors are aliens. They're half right.

Write a story using the words "failed mission," "moon" and "transplant."

Aliens begin invading rural communities, but their high-tech weapons are no match for the steel and dedication of a well-organised community of hardened farmers.

You were abandoned as a baby and sent through the

foster system. As you got older, you realised you were not like other kids. Now, though, you are finding it harder to keep your secret and people are beginning to get suspicious.

A hive mind alien invades Earth and you cannot tell who has been infected or not. Your only hope is to escape into the wilderness, but you can't do it alone.

Aliens sent a disease to cleanse Earth so they could terraform it. But some humans become far stronger for it. You are one of these humans, and the time has come to fight.

A family hide from an alien invasion in a storm shelter. Describe the first night.

A meteor hits Earth, delivering a deadly alien infection that quickly begins spreading. As a dropout college botanist, you think you might have accidentally discovered the cure. Is it too late?

The last man on Earth becomes the first man to make contact with an alien species.

The new space launch was disrupted by interference from deep space. Was it accidental, or on purpose? Are they friend, or foe?

Write a story that ends with the sentence: "We proved the conspiracy theories wrong. But we've uncovered something far worse."

A young girl on the Luna sanctuary finds an alien animal in need of help.

You discover something strange growing in your garden. Something not of this world.

A character who has made their living conjuring fake

conspiracy theories to rile up people online accidentally discovers one that is true.

It began when the homeless started going missing. We never imagined they were being abducted. We never imagined they would all return so very changed, either.

Aliens invade an isolated prison, but the prisoners are ready to fight back.

An ancient language translator makes a mistake on his latest piece and incorrectly decodes an alien message. Everything the world has ever known is about to change.

A woman shares an unforgettable night with an unknown man. A month later, she discovers that she is pregnant. This is no ordinary child.

You're a lifeguard at work when something unrecognisable comes out of the water onto the beach.

When it looked like the human race was doomed, they sent a call for help out to space. Something replied, but salvation came at a price.

A peaceful alien community is invaded by humans looking to claim resources from their planet.

Large machines land on Earth and begin destroying all technology in an attempt to return mankind to its humble beginnings.

An alien ship was shot down in Europe and is transported to Area 51 for examination. Write a story for the soldier accompanying it.

A group of children is abducted by aliens and taken

prisoner. While in captivity they bond with one of their capturers and plan an epic escape.

Humanoid aliens have lived among us in secrecy for many decades. Leaving their extra-terrestrial ways behind for generations, they've lived normal lives, and bred human/alien families. But this information has leaked, and now people are trying to discover who is hybrid and who is pure human.

While looking for alien life, Earth brought too much attention to itself. Now other species are coming. Some of them are not friendly.

Write a blog post from a man who was abducted three times, detailing his experiences.

A pharmacy is broken into overnight. When the owner goes to investigate, they find an injured alien woman passed out on the shop floor.

Hundreds of people who have been missing for decades all return to Earth. Slowly their families start to realise that whatever has returned isn't what they lost. It's something else, and it's dangerous.

A holy man believes he has found a way to communicate with his god, only to discover he's actually made first contact with an alien race.

A rip appears in space above Earth, and something is going to emerge from it.

A group of haggard old war veterans living in a retirement home are left to protect themselves and the other residents when the staff disappears during an alien invasion. Who knew they still had one last war to fight?

Aliens create an impenetrable force field around a little rural town. They have one goal in mind; To hunt.

There was a crash at Roswell, but the hostile aliens were met with fierce defiance from the locals in one great battle. Describe what the fight was like, and why the government kept it quiet.

Two planets are at war and our solar system is about to become the next battlefield.

A couple takes a weekend retreat away to try and fix their failing marriage when an alien ship lands in the woods next to them. Is this the adventure missing in their marriage?

The latest mission to space is on its return journey. And something is following them.

Plans to make the moon habitable have succeeded. But at what cost to what's already living there?

Your character was kidnapped by aliens and tortured

for years. They've now been returned to Earth. Can they return to the life they once knew? Do they want to?

They were sent to make peace with the aliens. Instead, they sold out the whole planet to save their own lives, and now they are on the run in the cosmos.

CHAPTER 10
HORROR AND ZOMBIES

A crew infected with a virus are forced to stay in orbit around earth until it clears their systems. But soon things take a turn for the weird.

Write a story that begins with the sentence: "We knew if we isolated the zombies, they would die out. And for a time we were right. Until they learned to reproduce."

There's something unknown in the rain, and the worst rainstorms in a generation are passing across America.

An infected man about to turn has a few hours to prepare his daughter to survive without him.

Write a story that begins with the sentence: "They weren't human and they were looking at me."

This new virus turns people into zombies. However, they remain unchanged, apart from a penchant for human flesh.

As part of a government experiment, four hundred people are locked inside "the dome," to live for twenty years. It all goes well for a time until something starts killing residents.

Write a story using the words "escape," "cabin" and "blood."

A pregnant woman struggles to keep herself, and her unborn baby, safe in a zombie apocalypse.

Death no longer means death in this world. And the victims of a mass murder are coming back for vengeance.

Returning from losing the championship match, a ladies hockey team bus is attacked. They must find a way to fight off the monsters. This is a victory they must achieve.

When the bombs hit, a man condemned to life in prison escapes the rubble of his holdings, only to discover there is not much of a world left.

A man on a stranded yacht in the middle of the ocean soon discovers something else is on board with him.

A teenage boy must hide the fact that he's a zombie from his classmates if he's ever to survive the school year.

A corporation ends the zombie outbreak by rounding up the infected and disposing of them efficiently. However, one journalist discovers the truth of what they are really doing. Can they get the story out?

Mushrooms that grow on zombies are the key to returning their humanity. But retrieving them is only the first problem.

You are working ground control, communicating with your team of astronauts on the new international space station. Problem is, the team keeps referring to a crew member who is not on the manifesto.

A retired army vet must keep his young family safe when there is a zombie outbreak at a ski resort.

You fall though into an underground cave system and discover something living down there.

A sudden high-pitched noise kills most of Earth's population. Only the hearing impaired survive.

People all over the world wake up to the horror that any child under six years old has disappeared.

In an abandoned farm outside of town, one man keeps his zombie wife chained up in the hopes he can cure her.

They call it "The Infected Show" and has been the number one programme on cable the last six months. One person in a room is infected. The people in there must figure out who it is and expel them before they all turn.

You move your young family into a new neighbourhood on Halloween weekend but there's something not quite right about it. It's just new house jitters, right?

A boy makes a robot bodyguard to protect him from his school bullies. One day, he loses control of the machine and the killings begin.

Once the zombie threat was neutralised, a detective must try to find out who was turned, who was killed and who was still missing.

A character gets a job in a small town known to have a massive monster problem. It's not perfect, but it's a pay cheque.

Write the diary of an old farmer living on his property with his young granddaughter, as they defend it from zombies.

The dead have returned, and are taking back their old lives by any means necessary.

Overnight, everyone disappears from a town. You have been sent in to the quarantine zone to discover the grisly truth.

You are a ghost, forced to watch your zombie body wander with the other hordes of the undead.

An old voodoo priest is causing a stir in prison and more and more prisoners are disappearing.

It started as a documentary chasing a myth, but it turned out that big foot should have remained a story. And remained undisturbed.

It turned out it wasn't tinnitus. They were hearing something no one else could.

Your character inherits an old house with a sealed-up room. Their first mistake was getting the crowbar.

An entire town reports that they can hear whispers. Then they begin dying one by one.

You are running from zombies. Write the character's internal dialogue.

A girl is attacked and left for dead in a forest. Three weeks later she wakes up where she was left, fully healed and incredibly hungry.

Those who live beyond the age of a hundred are now classed as zombies and killed on their birthday. You save your grandmother, but the day after her birthday something unexpected happens.

Zombies attack a kid's summer camp and a group of teen councillors have to lead the fight to protect them.

People say to never enter "No man's land," a stretch of desert with nothing for miles, except the creature that hunts there.

A great earthquake causes a crevice in the land and unleashes something.

The last of the zombies reside in water. The lack of oxygen and cold doesn't affect them. You make a living on a glass-bottomed boat. It's a safe, boring job. Usually.

Write a story using the sentence: "When I saw the first person change, I couldn't understand what I was seeing. Now I recognise it all too well."

In a monster-filled world, one of the nearby safe houses goes dark and you are sent to investigate.

Write a story using the words "shotgun," "farm" and "UFO."

A new alien houseplant becomes the new, must-have home accessory. Until one day, they all begin mutating.

An astronaut is attacked by insects on a planet visit. When he returns to the spaceship, they realise all too late that he has been infected.

A mother and daughter shopping trip takes a turn when zombies take over the mall.

Write a story that ends with the sentence: "He heard her screams grow silent and she was gone. All he could do was run."

Write a story from the point of view of a zombie who has been cured and is slowly rejoining society.

An astronaut is floating away from their spaceship after a space walk went wrong. Write about their last few minutes knowing it is the end.

Write a story using the words "hunted," "Egypt" and "curse."

A spaceship crash lands on a small town, unleashing a terrifying beast.

You live in a zombie apocalypse. But you have one trait that zombies don't benefit from; Luck.

Write the diary of the last man left alive on a space shuttle after a terrible attack.

After their boat sinks, a family takes refuge on an abandoned island. But they are not alone.

Write a story about a gang of teenagers enduring an eternity as socially awkward vampires.

Your character awakes inside a coffin.

Write a story that begins with the sentence: "I went to go check on our son. The crib was empty."

Write about a person as they run for their lives seeking an unlikely escape.

A strange circus has appeared just outside town but there's something sinister about its attractions.

Write a story that ends with the sentence: "His immortality would be the final curse. He would spend eternity screaming without anyone hearing him."

On a new space colony, a young child speaks of an imaginary friend. They soon discover they are quite real.

Something is hunting the elderly members of a community. Some seniors won't go down without a fight.

Write a story using the words "invasion," "pentagon" and "nuclear."

Write a day in the life of a soldier hired to clear zombies from a city.

Write a story using the sentence: "How was the same man he laughed with, drank with, now standing before him covered in blood?"

A character works at a check point during curfew, and she spots something alarming.

A fighter pilot spots something in the sky. Back at the barracks, no one believes him until it is too late.

The man tasked with finding the cure for the zombie apocalypse is experimenting on human subjects against their will.

Write a story using the sentence: "The days went on and I realised they were not coming back for me."

You work in the first class section of a cruise ship when there is an outbreak.

Write a story using the words "attack," "shadows" and "heartbreak."

A vampire gang kills the wrong man's daughter.

An artist uses zombies to create great works of art in an ethically questionable practice.

A man is doomed to relive the day he lost his entire family again and again. Is it a chance to avoid tragedy? Or is it a terrible punishment?

Write a story from the point of view of patient zero. It started with a cough.

A group of office workers are trapped in a small office building. Something outside is hunting them down one by one.

The dead return but one small town is ready to fight them back.

A child hides alone in his tree house, watching an invasion reach his neighbourhood.

Write a story that begins with the sentence: "The world ended because someone ate an animal mother nature did not want to be eaten."

Write a story using the words "scarecrow," "prom" and "Cadillac."

One day you hear strange noises coming from the apartment next door. It has been empty for months.

Write a story using the words "nano-bots," "destruction" and "spiders."

A man gets messages through his old AM radio from who he thinks is his deceased friend. He is wrong. It is something far worse.

One day, every child in a school collapses and goes into a coma, except for one unsettling girl.

Write a story using the sentence: "Without warning the birds suddenly started swarming overhead and attacking the zombies."

A strange creature walks the forest at night and a group of teenagers want to capture it on camera. Big mistake.

A young artist discovers that when she makes clay models of people, she can capture their soul.

A contagious airborne disease is released on a train crossing Europe.

Every day, more people from the colony go missing. It's your fault, but you can't control yourself.

Write a story using the sentence: "He handed me a knife, said I was on my own, and like that, my dad was gone."

Write the story of how a woman transforms into a monster.

An expedition of explorers discovers a large village full of dead bodies. But it's been abandoned for years.

An alien now haunts the forest where his ship crashed.

Write a story using the sentence: "My son had never been cut before. Never a scrape or nick. Now the blood that streamed from this small cut glowed amber in the light. What was he?"

They needed bodies for the invasion, but with no receptive human hosts, they had to look elsewhere.

A robbery goes wrong when the criminals break the chemical vial they were tasked with stealing and the team become infected.

Write a story using the words "chemical spill," "emergency room" and "disintegrate."

An unearthly mutation is making newborn babies rabid.

Ever since the electrical storm, an entire family has had the same unsettling nightmare.

A plane is haunted by ghosts who want today's passengers to suffer the same fate that they did.

Write a story using the sentence: "How can we fight an enemy we cannot see?"

A school must protect its students from a chemical outbreak. But what do they do when "infected" parents start storming the grounds demanding their kids back?

Write what the world after the zombie apocalypse is like. From resource gathering, to zombie fighting.

Children are suddenly going missing all across the globe, and there is no earthly reason behind their disappearance.

When zombies attack, the residents of a trailer park stand up to them with everything at their disposal.

A billionaire pays to access a quarantine zone and save his daughter left behind.

While exploring underwater caverns, biologists awaken something. And dry land will not keep it at bay.

A character is racing a countdown to escape an infected city before it becomes locked down.

THANK YOU FOR READING

Word of mouth is crucial for any author to succeed and honest reviews of my books help to bring them to the attention of other readers.

If you enjoyed this book, and have 2 minutes to spare, please leave it an honest review. Even if it's just a sentence or two it would make all the difference and would be very much appreciated.

Thank you.

ALSO BY JAN POWER

1000 Fantasy Writing Prompts

Beat your writers block, and kick start creativity with over 1000 fantasy writings prompts!

www.ingramcontent.com/pod-product-compliance
Lightning Source LLC
Chambersburg PA
CBHW040241130526
44590CB00049B/4065